GO WILD
ON THE
RIVER

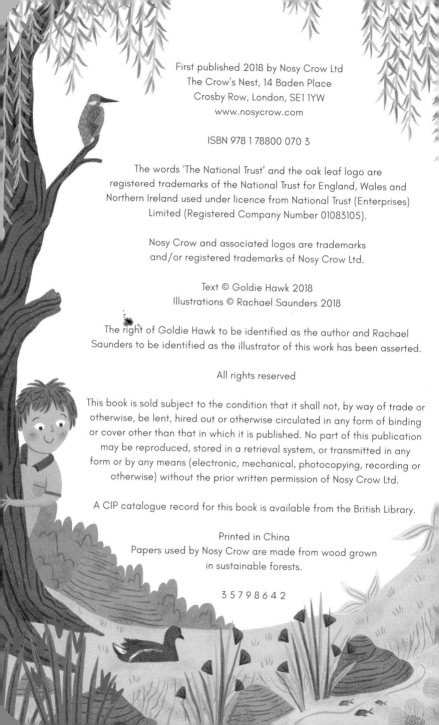

First published 2018 by Nosy Crow Ltd
The Crow's Nest, 14 Baden Place
Crosby Row, London, SE1 1YW
www.nosycrow.com

ISBN 978 1 78800 070 3

The words 'The National Trust' and the oak leaf logo are
registered trademarks of the National Trust for England, Wales and
Northern Ireland used under licence from National Trust (Enterprises)
Limited (Registered Company Number 01083105).

Nosy Crow and associated logos are trademarks
and/or registered trademarks of Nosy Crow Ltd.

Text © Goldie Hawk 2018
Illustrations © Rachael Saunders 2018

The right of Goldie Hawk to be identified as the author and Rachael
Saunders to be identified as the illustrator of this work has been asserted.

A CIP catalogue record for this book is available from the British Library.

Printed in China
Papers used by Nosy Crow are made from wood grown
in sustainable forests.

3 5 7 9 8 6 4 2

GO WILD
ON THE
RIVER

GOLDIE HAWK & RACHAEL SAUNDERS

nosy crow

NOTE TO GROWN-UPS

Grown-ups, be warned: this book contains sharp sticks, wild animals and waterfalls!

'What?!' we hear you say . . .

But we believe it's important to teach children how to do these things correctly and with due care. Along with our instructions, we've included plenty of reminders about safety. We know that you will supervise your children properly when engaging in these potentially dangerous activities, but we also hope that this book will encourage you to join in and rediscover the fun and magic of going

WILD ON THE RIVER!

Rivers are magical places and there's plenty of fun to be had — whether you discover the neon blue flash of a kingfisher or the spectacle of mayflies emerging on a May morning.

Using this book, you can create amazing memories playing pooh sticks, crossing stepping stones or river-dipping for all kinds of weird and wonderful water creatures. It will help you find your first grey heron standing still as a statue, a floating, jewelled dragonfly or bright yellow marsh marigolds.

So go on — it's time to get out into nature and enjoy the remarkable river!

GWEN POTTER — NATIONAL TRUST COUNTRYSIDE MANAGER

CONTENTS

ARE YOU READY TO GO WILD ON THE RIVER?

Do you love adventure, getting outdoors and making a splash? Then this is the book for you!

In this ultimate guide, you will find lots of fun activities to do on or around rivers, from finding animals and wildlife to sifting streams and building your own raft. You will also learn exactly what not to do, from standing on frozen water to slipping down a waterfall.

This book is about being safe and having fun. But it's also about having adventures. You should be willing to get a bit muddy and smelly and you absolutely must be good at working in a team.

There are three important rules for going wild on the river:
1. When in doubt, DON'T!
2. Always ask your grown-up.
3. Have fun!

LET'S GO WILD!

Always be careful, stick with an adult and don't push anyone in!

Rivers can be very dangerous. Riverbanks (the sides of rivers, not where fish keep their money!) are slippery and even if the water isn't deep, you don't want to end up soggy and cold.

WHAT IS A RIVER?

Rivers are pathways of fresh water (in other words, water that's not salty like the sea). Rivers can be big or small, wide or narrow, and sometimes two or more of them join together to create a really big river. They begin at a 'source', at the top of mountains or hills, and flow down to the 'mouth', which feeds into a sea or lake.

If a river is flowing very fast, this means it is close to the river source. If it is very slow and winding, this means it is close to the river mouth.

You often find big cities near the mouths of rivers. This is because people need water to drink and land full of nutrients from the river's flooding cycle for farming.

WHAT YOU WILL NEED ON THE RIVER

WHAT TO TAKE:

- A notebook and pencil
- A fishing net
- A bucket, plastic tray or jar
- A clear plastic cup (see page 17)
- Binoculars
- A magnifying glass
- A mobile phone (for emergencies)
- A map
- Duct tape
- A water-sifter (see pages 20-21)
- Snacks
- A towel
- First aid kit: scissors, bandages, antiseptic wipes, gauze, tape, blister plasters, safety pins, medical tape, hydrocortisone cream

WHAT NOT TO TAKE:
A tambourine, a hockey stick, your pet cat, knitting needles, a laptop.

WHAT TO WEAR:

- A T-shirt or long-sleeved top
- Comfortable trousers
- A jumper
- A warm coat
- A waterproof coat in case it rains
- Comfortable boots or wellies / sandals in the summer
- Warm socks (and some extra pairs!)
- A swimming costume or trunks
- A life jacket (if you're going on the water)

WHAT NOT TO WEAR:
A fish costume, a swanky suit, flippers, some jazzy jewellery.

FINDING OUT ABOUT RIVERS
FINDING THE DEPTH OF A RIVER

It's good to know how deep a river is in case you need to cross it or want to find out what kinds of creatures might be lurking beneath. To do so, you can create a special measuring tool:

1) Find a long, thin stick, around one metre long.

2) Tie a piece of string to the stick.

3) Tie a small stone to the string.

4) Let the stone fall into the water until it touches the bottom.

5) When you feel it touch the bottom, pull it back out.

6) The wet part of your string will show you how deep the river is.

7) If your stone doesn't hit the bottom, this means your river is very deep and you'll need a longer piece of string.

HOW NOT TO MEASURE THE DEPTH OF A RIVER:
By jumping in, by pushing your little brother in, by pushing anyone in.

HOW TO MEASURE HOW FAST A RIVER IS FLOWING

To measure the average flow of water, you will need someone to stand at a 'start' point with a float (e.g. a stick). Another member of your group should stand five metres along the riverbank, carrying a stopwatch. Try to find a section of river that is relatively straight so that you can measure with a tape measure in a straight line.

GOOD FLOATS TO USE:
A stick, a piece of driftwood.

1) On the count of three, the person at the start should drop their float into the river from a bridge or a riverbank.

2) The stopwatch-holder should start the clock as soon as the float drops into the water.

3) When the float reaches the five-metre mark, they must stop the stopwatch and record the time.

4) Do this another four or five times and record the time on the stopwatch each time.

5) Once you have all your times, add them up and divide by the number of times you launched your float – the final number is your average speed.

BAD FLOATS TO USE:
Your maths homework, your younger brother, your dog.

DID YOU KNOW...? RIVETING RIVER FACTS!

1. The longest river in the world is the Nile at 4,130 miles long.

2. Most of the water we drink comes from rivers that flow past our towns — it has to be cleaned very thoroughly before it reaches our taps, though!

3. The longest rivers in the UK are the Severn at 220 miles long and the Thames at 215 miles long.

4. Powerful rivers can carve out canyons in the landscape. The Grand Canyon in Arizona, USA was carved by a roaring river.

5. You can use rivers to create electricity — 24% of the world's electrical energy is currently created using hydroelectricity.

6. The Hudson River in New York is over a mile wide. In 2009, a US Airways plane managed to successfully land on the river after the plane was hit by birds, and everyone on board survived.

7. Some cities have 'urban beaches', which are actually at the edge of rivers.

8. Millions of people travel under rivers every day by taking underground trains.

9. A drop of rain that joins the River Thames at its source will go through eight people (drink, wee, flush) before reaching the sea.

HOW TO MAP A RIVER CORRIDOR

To explore and examine a river, you can map out a section of it. To do this, choose about 500 metres of a river and draw it out on a piece of paper. Next, create a key and note down all the different features of the river and the ground surrounding it.

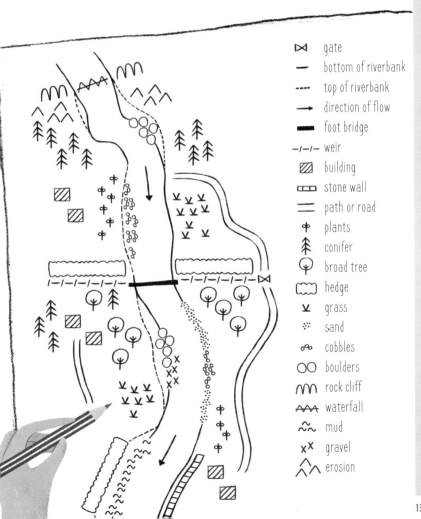

⋈	gate
—	bottom of riverbank
----	top of riverbank
→	direction of flow
▬	foot bridge
–/–/–	weir
▨	building
▭▭	stone wall
═	path or road
⚶	plants
⥯	conifer
⊕	broad tree
⌒⌒	hedge
⌄	grass
∴	sand
∘ᴼ	cobbles
∞	boulders
⋀⋀	rock cliff
⋀⋀⋀	waterfall
∼∼	mud
×ˣ	gravel
∧∧	erosion

RIVER
CROW

	mud		camping area		hedge
	sand		conifers		stone wall
	boulders				wooden gate
	cobbles		trees		path
			reeds		bridge
					fence
					building

(This map is not to scale — it's just for fun!)

15

WATERFALLS

Waterfalls are places in the river where water suddenly flows down a steep cliff into a pool below. Waterfalls can be big or small and they usually develop because of erosion, where the water wears away soft rock, leaving only the hard rock.

Waterfalls are really beautiful and great fun to explore, as long as you remain safe. The pools below can be shallow or deep and there may be rocks below the surface, so never jump in.

The largest waterfall in the world is Angel Falls in Venezuela. It is 979 metres tall, which is more than ten times the height of Big Ben in London!

DID YOU KNOW?
During the rainy season, so much water falls over the Iguacu Falls in South America that it could fill six Olympic-sized swimming pools every second!

HOW TO MEASURE THE QUALITY OF THE WATER

For fish to survive and river wildlife to grow, there must be good-quality water. This is also essential for us, because we use water from rivers to drink and grow our food. Sadly, river water can be polluted by rubbish or by chemicals used on farms and in factories.

If a river is healthy, it will be moving – the colour of the water will not be too dark and there will be lots of river wildlife, including fish and insects.

Take a clear plastic cup and fill it with a sample of river water. Is the water clear or murky? What colour does it match on the scale above?

■ ■ ■ ■ ■ □ ■ ■ ■ ■ ■ ■ ■ ■

Acidic   Neutral   Alkaline

REMEMBER:
Weather can affect the colour of the water. If it's been raining recently, it might be darker because of all the silt and mud that's been washed down it.

You can also discover how acidic the water is by dipping in special litmus paper and checking the colour against this scale.

THE WATER CYCLE

The water we get from our taps has been recycled again and again for more than four billion years — so the water you drink today could be the same water dinosaurs drank long ago! In that time, it's constantly changed from water to gas to ice and has moved from lakes to rivers to oceans to the ground.

1) EVAPORATION

Heat from the sun warms up water, which then 'evaporates' by turning into 'water vapour' (an invisible gas). Some water evaporates from the leaves of plants — this is called 'transpiration'.

2) CONDENSATION

The water vapour rises into the sky and, as it gets higher, it cools down and becomes a liquid again. This is a process called 'condensation'. All these condensed water droplets turn into clouds, so if you went through a cloud, you would end up very soggy!

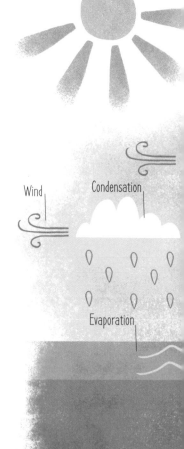

Wind

Condensation

Evaporation

3) PRECIPITATION

Soon, the water droplets in the clouds get bigger and become too heavy for the air. They turn into rain or snow, and take the long journey back down to Earth.

4) COLLECTION

All of this fallen water lands on Earth, either in lakes, rivers or oceans or on solid ground, where it will start the cycle all over again! This is called 'collection'. Some water might soak into the ground or be taken up by plant roots. In very cold places, water might collect as snow, ice, or even glaciers. When temperatures rise, this will melt back into water and flow into rivers or oceans.

Precipitation —

Collection

WHAT TO DO ON THE RIVER
HOW TO SIFT A STREAM

There are lots of things running through a river and to find out what they are, you can make a special sifting tool. A sifter is a bit like a sieve – it lets the water run through the thin mesh holes, but traps everything else.

WHAT YOU MIGHT CATCH:
Weeds, sticklebacks, minnows, river snails, sediment, small pebbles, sand.

YOU WILL NEED:

• A wire coat hanger or a strong piece of wire
• Some mesh or netting (a woven material with tiny holes to allow water through)
• Some duct tape

METHOD:

1) Create a circle with your wire coat hanger or piece of wire.

2) Place your mesh over the circle and fold over the edges.

3) Stick your mesh in place using duct tape.

4) Find your stream and, with help from your grown-up, place your sifter in the water.

5) Take your sifter out of the stream and see if it has collected anything.

6) Note down your discoveries – if you can't recognise something, draw a sketch and you can look it up later.

WHAT YOU WILL PROBABLY NOT CATCH:
A big fish, an old boot, a beaver, pieces of gold (but well done if you do!).

How to Play Pooh Sticks

This is a super-fun game to play with your friends and one that might seem simple, but requires good throwing and stick-finding skills. The 'pooh' comes from *Winnie the Pooh*, the book series in which it was invented – don't worry, there's no poo involved!

1) Find a bridge over moving water.

2) Everyone must find a stick – to remember which is yours, pick one with a distinctive shape.

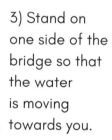

3) Stand on one side of the bridge so that the water is moving towards you.

4) On the count of three, drop your sticks into the stream.

5) Run to the other side of the bridge.

REMEMBER:
You'll win if you pick a spot where the water is running faster!
(See page 10)

6) The stick that floats out first is the winning stick! If you get really good at this, you can take part in the world pooh-sticks championship – yes, it exists!

HOW TO SKIM STONES

Skimming stones is a fun game to play with your friends and takes a lot of practice.

To be a stone-skimming pro, you need the perfect stone. It needs to be thin, flat, palm-sized and very light. And the smoother it is, the better it will skim. Slate is the best kind of stone for skimming.

You also need a calm river, with a safe riverbed to stand on so you don't fall over.

REMEMBER:
Don't skim stones
if there are any birds
(or any of your friends)
in the water!

1) Hold the stone with your strongest hand, so that the stone is on top of your middle finger and underneath your thumb and forefinger.

2) Bend your knees and look at the point you want to throw towards.

3) Throw the stone straight out towards the river and watch it skim. Use your thumb and forefinger to add spin as you throw.

It may take a bit of practice, but soon you'll be a champion skimmer!

DID YOU KNOW?
The world record for the highest number of stone skims is 88!

How to Build a Mini Raft

You Will Need:

- Four thick sticks of equal length for your frame
- Around eight to ten thin twigs
- String or strong grass
- A good leaf for your sail

Method:

1) Take your four thick sticks and place them in a square shape.

WHAT YOU WILL NOT NEED:
A remote control, decorative pom-poms, a pirate flag, an on-board catapult to destroy other rafts (that would not be good sportsmanship).

2) Using string or grass, tie these sticks together.

3) Take all but one of your thin twigs and fix them to your frame using string or grass.

4) Use your leftover twig as a mast and wedge this in between your other twigs, with a leaf attached to it for your sail.

HOW TO BUILD A LOG RAFT

You can create a larger raft using logs. All you need is six logs of a similar size, six slightly longer wooden poles and some strong rope.

1) Place your logs next to each other in a shallow patch of water where they can float – make sure there isn't a current or they will set sail by themselves!

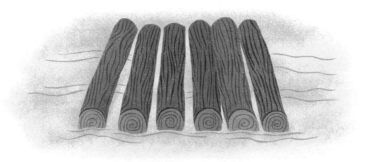

2) Place three of your wooden poles underneath these logs (one at the top of the logs, one in the middle and one at the bottom).

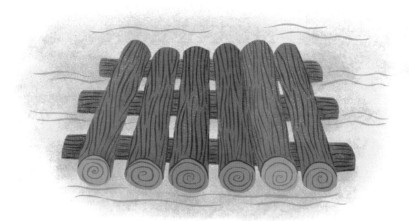

3) Place the other three wooden poles on top of your logs in the same positions as the poles below.

4) Tie the ends of the wooden poles together tightly to secure the logs in between – start with a clove hitch knot (see page 32) and then lash your rope around each end.

DID YOU KNOW?
Every year, on 30th April in Uppsala, Sweden, hundreds of local students build large rafts and float down the Fyris River to celebrate the Valborg festival.

How to Build a Barrel Raft

You can create a barrel raft, which floats brilliantly well, with just eight sturdy wooden poles (four long, four slightly shorter), four large watertight plastic barrels and some strong rope. All you need to do is:

1) Lay your four long poles out on the ground parallel to each other – there should be 40 cm between poles 1 and 2, 80 cm between poles 2 and 3, and 40 cm between poles 3 and 4.

2) Tie these poles together tightly where they cross, using your rope – start with a clove hitch knot (see page 32) on one arm of the X and then lash the rope around the other sides.

3) Tie your barrels to each corner, wrapping the rope around them.

4) Now you're ready to go!

HOW TO TIE A CLOVE HITCH KNOT

This is a great knot when you need to tie something to a tree, stick or pole.

1) Wrap one end of the rope around the tree, stick or pole.

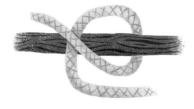

2) Cross this end up and over the wrapped part of the rope, so that it forms an X shape.

3) Loop the end over the pole once more.

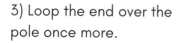

4) As you bring the end of the rope back up, tuck it underneath the rope, creating another X. Pull tight.

HOW TO MAKE STEPPING STONES

Find a shallow stream and look for some large, sturdy stones. Place them in the bed of the stream and push down to make sure they're dug in securely.

Now you can carefully step over the stones without getting wet!

WHAT NOT TO DO ON STEPPING STONES:
Practise your dance moves, play hopscotch on them, give someone a piggyback.

SURVIVAL TIP
Make sure you check what lies downstream — you don't want to accidentally head towards a waterfall!

HOW TO MAKE A PAPER BOAT

1) Fold a rectangular piece of paper in half.

2) Unfold and fold in half again downwards.

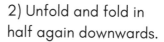

3) Fold in the corners.

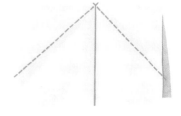

4) Fold up the edges on both sides.

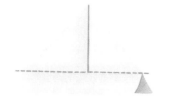

5) Pull the sides apart from the bottom and flatten. Tuck one side under the other.

6) Fold the front and back layers up.

REMEMBER:
When using paper, don't forget to remove it from the water before you leave!

7) Pull the sides apart from the bottom and flatten.

8) Pull the top flaps outwards.

9) Squish the bottom and pull the sides up.

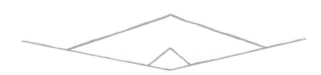

Now, race your boats along a river or a stream and see which one wins.

HOW TO GO KAYAKING

Going kayaking is a great way to explore rivers. All you need is a kayak, a grown-up and a gentle river – you don't want too big a current or you might end up capsizing.

1) Carefully get into your kayak – try not to fall in. (That would be *oarful*!)

2) Hold your paddle with a light grip, so that your knuckles are in line with the blades.

3) Move through the water by dipping your paddle into the water on your right side and pushing the water away from you, then do the same on your left side.

4) If you want to veer left, paddle more on your right side; if you want to veer right, paddle more on your left.

WHAT NOT TO DO ON YOUR KAYAK:
Practise your dance moves, do a spot of yoga, play musical chairs, paddle towards a waterfall. (This might sound fun, but you probably won't live to tell the tale!)

BOATS

ROWING BOAT

A rowing boat is a small boat, with one or more people using oars to move through the water. Rowing races date back to ancient Egypt and Rome!

DINGHY

A dinghy is a small boat used for sailing. Wind hits the sails and pushes the boat along, while the rudder and tiller are used for steering.

PADDLEBOARD

A paddleboard is a bit like a long surfboard, which you stand or kneel on, while using an oar to move through the water. You need good balance to travel on one of these!

NARROWBOAT

A narrowboat is long and, unsurprisingly, rather narrow. They were originally used for carrying goods along canals, but are now used as homes or just for a fun day out on the water.

PUNT

A punt is a small, rectangular boat with a flat bottom. They are used in small rivers or canals and the driver (or 'punter') carries a long pole, which they use to propel the boat along and to steer with.

BANANA BOAT

A banana boat is shaped like a banana and is pulled along by a speedboat. It is probably not the most practical when it comes to travelling across a river, unless you want to fall in!

LEARN SOME NAUTICAL LINGO

BUOY – a float in the water to which boats can be moored

BOW – the front of a boat

CAPSIZE – when a boat tips over in the water

LEEWARD – the direction away from the wind

MOORING – securing your boat to a buoy or a pier

PORT – the left side of the boat

SKIPPER – the captain of the boat

STARBOARD – the right side of the boat

STERN – the back of a boat

WINDWARD – the direction towards the wind

HOW TO MAKE A FISHING ROD

REMEMBER:
You can't just fish anywhere. In lots of rivers, fish are protected, so make sure you do your research and ask permission first.

1) Find a long, straight wooden pole or stick, around five or six feet long.

2) Cut a little notch on one end and tie some fishing line around it.

3) Attach a fishing hook to the end of the line with a knot.

4) Add some bait, like an earthworm, a maggot or a bit of bread, to the hook. Adding a weight will also help.

5) To find out how to use your rod to catch a fish, turn to the next page . . .

HOW TO GO FISHING

Before you go fishing, you need to find the perfect spot. It should be somewhere with lots of fish, clean water and a place where you're happy to spend a long time. And no, you can't just fish anywhere. Lots of good fishing spots are privately owned so make sure you have permission first.

1) Cast your line by bringing the rod to your side and then swinging it smoothly in the direction you want to fish in. (Try to avoid whacking anyone in the process!)

REMEMBER:
To go fishing, anyone over the age of 12 will need a rod licence. Find out more at: www.gov.uk/fishing-licences

2) Wait quietly – fish are startled by loud noise, so don't be tempted to sing or put a radio on!

3) If you feel or see the rod jerk, you might have a bite – reel the line back in and see what you've caught.

4) If you don't feel a bite after 10–15 minutes, reel in your line and cast it again.

Fishing takes a lot of practice, but keep at it and you'll soon pick it up.

HOW TO PREPARE FISH FOR COOKING

Before cooking a fish, you need to gut it so it's safe (and tasty!) to eat. You will need clean water, a sharp knife and your grown-up to help you out. To gut your fish:

1) Wash the fish thoroughly in clean, cold water.

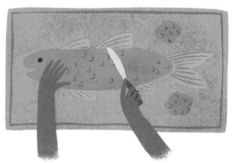

2) Scrape off any scales by rubbing the blunt side of your knife from the tail towards the head of the fish.

3) Turn the fish on its side and cut off its head and gills.

46

4) Keeping the fish on its side, cut a slit from the belly at the tail end to the head.

5) Pull out all the guts and roe (fish eggs).

6) Cut off the fins and the tail.

7) Wash the fish (inside and out) once more, rinsing off all the leftover blood with cold, running water.

8) Your fish is now ready to be cooked.

INGREDIENTS THAT MIGHT MAKE YOUR FISH EVEN TASTIER:
Salt, pepper, lemon, butter, mixed herbs.

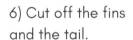

HOW TO BUILD A DAM

Dams are built to control the amount of water flowing through a river. Sometimes these are made by humans to create large lakes called reservoirs. The water in a reservoir is used in houses, factories and on farms.

Beavers also build dams to create protection from predators and to build a safe store for their food. They use their powerful teeth to gnaw down branches and carry twigs and stones in their paws.

METHOD:

1) Collect logs, sticks, stones, gravel and mud.
2) Place the logs and larger stones across a shallow stream.
3) Add the smaller sticks, stones and mud.

REMEMBER:
Always remove the dam before you leave. Have fun smashing it down when you've finished — this will be easier if it's not too deep!

Now your dam is built, check for any wildlife in the empty riverbed. Gently return anything that you find to the water on the far side of your dam.

HOW TO MAKE A TYRE SWING

If you find a strong, healthy tree by a riverbank and you have permission, why not make a tyre swing? They're a great way to have fun by the river . . . but don't get too tired out or you might end up feeling a bit ropey!

TOP TIP
If you're setting up a swing over a river, be sure to check how deep the water is first. Look out for any rocks under the surface, too.

YOU WILL NEED:

- A tyre
- Some long, thick, heavy-duty rope
- A strong, healthy tree on a riverbank
- A tall grown-up to help you set it up

METHOD:

1) Give your tyre a good clean to remove any dirt or oil.

2) Get your grown-up to climb up a ladder and tie the rope around your tree branch, using a bowline knot. Make sure the knot is nice and solid.

SURVIVAL TIP
The tree branch has to be healthy — avoid any branches with cracks or signs of disease. Otherwise, you might be in for a bumpy (and very wet) surprise!

HOW TO TIE A BOWLINE KNOT

1)

2)

3)

4)

3) Work out how far off the ground you would like the tyre to hang: not too low or your legs will drag on the ground when you swing, but not too high or you won't be able to climb on to it in the first place.

4) Tie the other end of the knot to the top of the tyre, using another bowline knot.

5) Trim off any excess rope.

REMEMBER:
Always remove
the swing before
you leave.

6) Test your swing
— if it works, get
swinging!

53

WHAT TO SEE ON THE RIVER

There's so much for you to spot in and around rivers if you look carefully. Lots of animals go to rivers to drink, eat or swim, so go with the flow and see what you can find.

Why not try dipping your fishing net into the water? Swirl it around for ten seconds, then pull it out and tip what you've caught in a bucket, a plastic tray or a jar filled with pond water. But remember to put everything back where you find it! However much you might want a pet newt, it might not be very happy about being taken from its habitat.

WILD ANIMALS TO SPOT — FISH

TROUT

Trout swim in fast-flowing water because they are very active and need lots of oxygen.

CRAYFISH AND SHRIMP

Freshwater crayfish and shrimp like to sit at the bottom of the river and are most active at night.

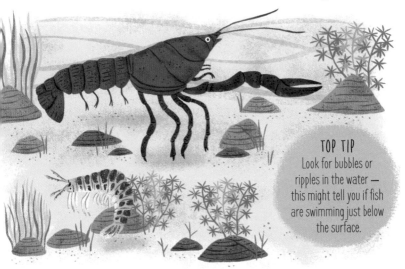

TOP TIP
Look for bubbles or ripples in the water — this might tell you if fish are swimming just below the surface.

PERCH

Perch are predators and like to stay on the bottom of the river, hidden by the weeds.

PIKE

Pike are predators and can grow up to three feet long. They like to stay on the bottom of the river, hidden by the weeds and ready to pounce.

CARP

Carp like higher temperatures so they swim in shallow, slow-flowing water.

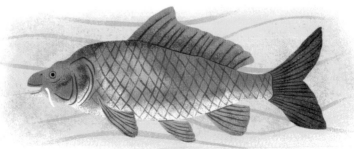

STICKLEBACKS

Sticklebacks are very small with little spines and are often eaten by bigger fish and water birds.

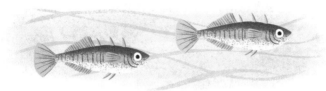

MINNOWS

Minnows are even smaller fish. They swim in shallow water and are good at hiding from predators.

SALMON

Salmon are born in rivers, migrate to saltwater and then come back to rivers to lay their eggs in the riverbed.

EELS

Eels are long and snake-like with slimy skin. No one really knows for certain, but it is believed that they are born in the Sargasso Sea and reach UK rivers after three years. Eels can live to be 100 years old!

AMPHIBIANS
NEWTS

Newts are very slender with a brown-green colour, often covered in black spots and with an orange belly. They are nocturnal and spend the day hiding under stones or earth.

FROGS

Frogs are born as frogspawn, which are lots of little eggs that float on the top of slow-moving water. They then become tadpoles and swim around. Over six to nine weeks, tadpoles grow, lose their tails, develop legs and their gills become lungs. Finally, they become frogs.

DID YOU KNOW?
If you kiss a frog, it is more likely to make your lips itch than to turn into a prince!

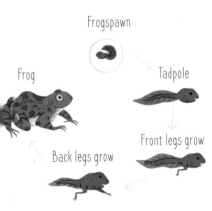

Frogspawn

Frog

Tadpole

Front legs grow

Back legs grow

To spot a frog, listen out! Male frogs croak to attract female frogs. The best time to hear them is during the mating season (between January and March) and after it has rained a lot – this is when they are most active.

WATER BIRDS

HERONS

Herons are expert fishers. They have long legs and a long, thin neck. To catch fish, they stand very tall and still, curve their neck, then suddenly straighten it, stabbing the fish with their long, pointy beak.

CORMORANTS

Cormorants are large and black with white cheeks. They often stand with their wings held out to dry and are excellent fishers, eating eels, small fish and even water snakes.

MALLARDS

Mallards are the most common duck and they feed on plants and insects. Males are grey with a green head, yellow bill, white neckband and curly black tail feathers. Females are brown and black with an orange bill. You might spot a mallard in the water with its bottom in the air – this is called 'upending' and is how ducks catch their food.

KINGFISHERS

Kingfishers are small birds with bright blue and orange feathers. They are also excellent at catching fish and they create single burrows, high up in the riverbank. To spot these burrows, look for white splashes at the entrance — these are their droppings.

SAND MARTINS

Sand martins are small and brown, with white underparts and a brown band across their chest. They eat small insects and create clusters of burrows in riverbanks because they breed in groups.

CRANES

Cranes are large birds with long legs, a long neck and drooping, curved tail feathers. They build nests in shallow water and often walk in circles, bobbing around as if they're dancing.

MOORHENS

Moorhens are blackish-brown above and grey below, with a red beak. They twitch their neck and tail and are very territorial during breeding season. They find food on the surface of the water or on land.

COOTS

Coots are closely related to moorhens, but are black with a white beak. They build nests in shallow water and are very territorial during breeding season. They dive up to two metres below the surface for food.

SWANS

Swans are bright white, with a long S-shaped neck and an orange-black bill. The swan population has increased in the UK recently, partly because they are protected birds. In fact, all unmarked swans on the Thames actually belong to the Queen!

GREYLAG GEESE

Greylag geese look a bit like swans but with mottled grey feathers. They mainly eat grass and often make cackling, honking noises. If they're angry, they might even hiss.

MAMMALS
OTTERS

Otters are sensitive and shy animals, so you will be lucky to spot one. Your best chance is in the early morning. Their webbed feet, long thick tails and streamlined bodies make them excellent swimmers, and they can hold their breath underwater for four minutes!

BEAVERS

Beavers are very rare, but the best time to spot them is at dusk or dawn, when they are most active. They are brilliant at building dams and cutting wood between their big front teeth.

WATER VOLES

Water voles make burrows in riverbanks, with entrances above and below the water. To spot one, look out for these holes when the water levels are low. You might also find some clues around the holes, such as plants that have been nibbled diagonally and black droppings with rounded ends.

WATER SNAILS

Water snails look a bit like normal snails you see in the garden, but they live in slow-moving rivers or around the shores of lakes. They feed on algae and are sometimes put in garden ponds to keep the water clean.

INSECTS
POND SKATERS

Pond skaters look like they are rowing over the water, as they use their middle pair of legs to push themselves forward, and their back ones to steer.

DID YOU KNOW?
Dragonflies existed around 70 million years before dinosaurs!

WATER BOATMEN

Water boatmen swim on their backs, using their strong hind legs to paddle and their short front legs to catch their food.

DAMSELFLIES AND DRAGONFLIES

Damselflies and dragonflies fly gracefully above the surface of rivers, eating smaller insects.

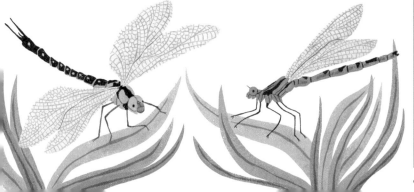

TREES AND FLOWERS TO SPOT

ALDER

An alder is a conical-shaped tree,
which can grow up to 25 metres,
has dark-green, leathery leaves
with flat ends, and can be
easily spotted by its
flowers (cylinder catkins)
and fruit (woody cones).

WEEPING WILLOW

There are various
different types
of willow tree,
but this weeping willow,
often seen along rivers, is a
hybrid between the white
willow and the true
weeping willow (which is
very rare in Europe). Its
roots take oxygen and
nutrients up from water, so
they survive in very wet earth,
unlike most other trees.

WATER LILY

Water lilies float on the
surface of the water,
taking nutrients up
through roots at
the bottom.

BOGBEAN

Bogbeans can be found in
shallow, slow-moving water,
held up by floating stems.

BLADDERWORT

Bladderworts have no roots
and float around freely,
trapping water fleas and
other insects in their leaves.

WATER PARSNIP

Water parsnips have white, umbrella-shaped flower heads and grow on the banks of quiet water downstream.

MARSH MARIGOLD

Marsh marigolds have bright yellow flowers.

WATER CROWFOOT

Water crowfoot are dainty white flowers, with a yellow base on the petals.

GREAT REEDMACE

Also known as the bulrush, great reedmace has long leaves and tall stems with sausage-like flower heads.

WATER FIGWORT

Water figworts have small, round maroon flowers and square-shaped stems.

WATER FORGET-ME-NOT

Water forget-me-nots have sky-blue petals, with yellow middles.

WILD WEATHER
FLOODING

A flood happens when so much water falls into the river that it overflows. This is usually because it has been raining heavily, but it might be because a nearby dam has burst. In some continents, floods happen because of tidal waves or melting snow.

Floods can be very bad for farmers because they kill crops. But for bird-spotters they're exciting times because birds like waterfowl and waders appear in fields.

REMEMBER:
Don't ever try swimming in flood water — there could be dangerous currents, fast-floating objects or even sewage.

FREEZING

Have you ever seen a river freeze over? Back in the 17th and 18th centuries, the River Thames completely froze over and winter fairs, called 'frost fairs', were held on it. Small children played football on the ice and there were puppet shows, plays and horse-and-coach races.

Nowadays, it's not very common for a river to freeze over and, if it does, the ice is likely to be too thin to walk on. Large rivers rarely freeze completely because ice and snow are good insulators and keep the water below warmer than the temperature on top.

For birds, a freeze can be a problem because they can be cut off from their food supply. Often, they will fly to new areas in search of natural food like berries and seeds.

REMEMBER:
Never stand on a frozen river — no matter how thick the ice looks.

WHAT TO DO IF YOU GET INTO TROUBLE ON THE RIVER

Some rivers are fine to swim in and are perfect for a warm summer's dip, but others are very dangerous, even for strong swimmers. You must be careful when swimming in the wild. Always go with an adult and make sure you have researched the area.

CHECKLIST:

- ☐ Only swim in a designated swimming river.
- ☐ Make sure you have permission to swim there.
- ☐ Never swim without your grown-up.
- ☐ Check the water is not too deep.
- ☐ Check for rocks or branches beneath the surface.
- ☐ Avoid swimming after heavy rainfall.
- ☐ Do not swim in warm, slow-moving, stagnant water.

And, most importantly of all, no matter how good a swimmer you are, always take a life jacket and make sure you're with a grown-up.

IF SOMEONE FALLS IN (LIFE-SAVING SKILLS)

If a member of your team falls into the river, don't jump in and join them or you could quickly get into trouble, too! Try to pull them back in with a piece of rope, a float or a sturdy stick. Tell them to remain calm and not to panic. Then call for help.

CURRENTS

Sometimes, rivers can appear nice and calm but have a very strong current underneath. A current is the flow of water in a river and they tend to be stronger after it's been raining. If you get stuck in a current and it starts to sweep you away, remember to remain calm. If you panic and flap your arms about, you'll waste all your energy and you may push yourself underwater. Instead, take even breaths, remain floating and try to swim diagonally to the shoreline (not straight or you will swim against the current), while calmly calling to a member of your team for help.

EDDIES

An eddy might sound like a friendly person, but it is actually a patch of water with a swirling current. Eddies usually appear after the flow of water meets a big rock in the river, and you might be able to spot them by looking out for small whirlpools on the surface of the water.

HOW TO WADE THROUGH A RIVER

If you're in an emergency and have to wade through a river, you need to know how to do it correctly or you might find yourself in even more trouble.

1) First of all, assess the water you need to cross. How deep is it? Are there any rocks or plants blocking your path? How strong is the current? How cold is the water? Is there a better, shallower place to cross from?

2) After measuring the depth of the water (see page 8), check that your bag is waterproofed (you can put a bin liner over it if it isn't) and locate your wading staff – a sturdy, smooth stick that comes up to your shoulders is perfect. This will help you to keep your balance and make you look like a pro.

SURVIVAL TIP
Never wade through water that goes higher than your knees.

3) As you step into the water, use your stick to check for anything hidden under the surface — even in shallow water, rocks and branches might be lurking. Next, make slow, sideways shuffle-steps diagonally upstream. Don't try to do this quickly or you may lose your footing.

4) If you lose your footing and fall in, try to remain calm. Let the water take you (you'll lose energy if you struggle against it) and lie on your back with your feet facing downstream. Float with the current until you reach a shallow spot where you can stand again.

HOW NOT TO WADE THROUGH A RIVER:
Quickly, doing the conga, as a race, impersonating your dog.

HOW TO REMOVE LEECHES

Leeches look a bit like slugs, but they lurk in wet places and latch on to your skin. They suck blood from you, but you'll be glad to know that they're not usually very harmful. They are attracted to your smell, so to avoid them, use insect repellent and keep your skin covered by clothing.

If you do find one (or more!) on you, all you need to do is:

1) Look for the thinner end of the leech and scrape it off using your fingernail.

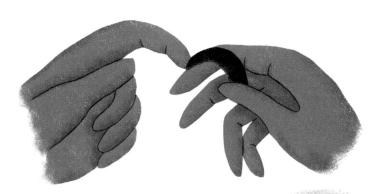

2) Use your fingernail to unstick the fat end too.

3) Flick the leech away once it is dislodged, but be careful — they're good at re-sticking themselves!

HOW NOT TO REMOVE A LEECH:
by shouting at it, by shaking it off (they're stronger than you think), by trying to wrench it off (its jaws might get left in your skin), by burning it, by pouring salt on it.

RIVER DISEASES

Rivers can be fun, but they can also make you very ill, especially if you're swimming in tropical rivers. Here are some dangerous diseases you can catch near rivers.

MALARIA

If you have malaria, you will have a bad fever, a very high temperature, headaches, sweating, and — in particularly awful cases — you might die. It's caused by malarial mosquitos, which lay their eggs on the river. Luckily, you're very unlikely to catch it in the UK, but if you are near a hot, swampy river, make sure you cover yourself in mosquito spray.

RIVER BLINDNESS

River blindness causes very itchy skin and damages your eyesight. It happens when tropical blackflies bite you and spit tiny grubs into your blood. These grubs then turn into worms, which lay their eggs and hatch into lots more worms. They then spread through your body and can blind you if they reach your eyes.

WEIL'S DISEASE

Weil's disease gives you very bad muscle pain, diarrhoea, headaches and vomiting. It is spread by the wee of rats, foxes, rabbits, cats and even hedgehogs! This is one of the only diseases you are likely to get in UK rivers. To avoid it, keep your mouth shut when swimming!

BILHARZIA

You might have bilharzia if you get a very itchy rash, a fever, chills, aches or pains and have been swimming in a tropical river. It is caused by tiny grub worms that live inside tropical river snails. They can lay their eggs inside your blood by burrowing into your skin.

CHOLERA

Cholera gives you extremely bad diarrhoea and vomiting, which makes you very dehydrated. You can catch it by drinking bad water . . . so if you fall in a river, remember to keep your mouth shut!

HOW NOT TO CATCH A RIVER DISEASE:
Keep cuts and grazes covered with a waterproof plaster, don't drink river water, wash your hands before eating.

RIVER QUIZ

1) What is the longest river in the world?
  - A: The Amazon
  - B: The Nile
  - C: The Ganges

2) What is the technical word for the right side of the boat?
  - A: Stern
  - B: Port
  - C: Starboard

3) In the water cycle, what word is used for heat warming up the water and turning it into water vapour?
  - A: Precipitation
  - B: Condensation
  - C: Evaporation

4) What is the name of the water disease that is caused by tiny grub worms that live inside tropical river snails?
  - A: Bilharzia
  - B: Cholera
  - C: Malaria

5) Which river insect swims on its back?
  - A: Pond skater
  - B: Dragonfly
  - C: Water boatman

6) What is the name for a small, rectangular-shaped boat, used in small rivers or canals, driven using a long pole?

> A: Rowing boat
>
> B: Punt
>
> C: Dinghy

7) What is the technical word for using water to create electricity?

> A: Hydroelectricity
>
> B: Geothermal electricity
>
> C: Aquapower

8) What ferocious fish with razor-sharp teeth lives in the Amazon river?

> A: Piranha
>
> B: Foot-snapper
>
> C: Barracuda

9) Which animal builds dams in rivers?

> A: Otter
>
> B: Moorhen
>
> C: Beaver

10) What is the name of the black water bird that often stands with its wings held out to dry?

> A: Cormorant
>
> B: Kingfisher
>
> C: Coot

ANSWERS: 1) The Nile 2) Starboard 3) Evaporation 4) Bilharzia 5) Water boatman 6) Punt 7) Hydroelectricity 8) Piranhas 9) Beaver 10) Cormorant

RIVER RESPECT

We hope you have a wonderful time on the river.
They can be magical places, whether you're
watching a dragonfly flitting over the surface,
or tracking a carp swimming through the water.

While it's great fun to go wild on the river, it's most
important to be respectful of this beautiful space.
That means following the rules, listening
to your grown-ups and being careful
not to disturb the environment. As the
saying goes, you should leave only
footprints and take only memories!

GLOSSARY

Amphibians
Cold-blooded animals that can live on land or water, but have to lay their eggs in water.

Current
The directed, flowing movement of water in a stream, river or sea.

Dam
A barrier that stops or reduces the flow of water. They can be made by humans or animals.

Downstream
A word to describe the direction in which a river or stream is flowing.

Driftwood
Wood that has been washed up on a beach, shore or bank from the water.

Fishing weight
A weight used to help a fishing line go further and sink deeper in the water.

Freshwater
Water that occurs naturally, and is found in lakes, streams and rivers as well as underground. It contains very little salt, but it is not the same thing as drinking water.

Glacier
A land-based body of thick ice that constantly moves under its own weight.

Life jacket
A sleeveless vest that can keep a person afloat in water.

Litmus paper

Filter paper that has been soaked with dyes, and can test water quality. Blue litmus paper turns red in acidic conditions, and red litmus paper turns blue in alkaline conditions.

Mammals

Warm-blooded animals with hair and a spine or backbone. Humans are mammals.

Mouth

The mouth of a river is the place where the river ends its journey and flows into a larger body of water.

Pollution

The dirtying of water by harmful pollutants. The polluted water carries diseases and can cause harm to humans and animals.

River corridor

The land that surrounds a river as it meanders along its journey.

Saltwater

Water that comes from a sea or an ocean.

Sediment

The mixture of sand and dirt that settles at the bottom of a river or lake.

Source

The source of a river is the point where the river begins to flow.

Upstream

A word to describe the direction opposite to the flow of a river or stream.

Water quality

The way we measure the condition of water, usually to check if it is suitable for drinking or swimming.

INDEX